Electronic and Information Technology Accessibility And IT Asset Management (ITAM)

NASA Technical Reports Server (NTRS), Roger H. Liang

IT Asset Management Working Group Meeting

Electronic and Information

Technology Accessibility

And

IT Asset Management (ITAM)

KSC

Roger H. Liang

Information Technology and Communication Services Directorate

l

Agenda

- Purpose
- Rehabilitation Action of 1973
- Rehabilitation Action of 1973 and NASA
- Kennedy Space Center History
- Agency Policy Requirements
- Assistive Technology and Disability Types
- Accessibility Notion
- Notional View of the Accessibility Space at KSC
- Section 508 Applicability to ITAM activities
- Back-up charts

2

Purpose

To discuss and understand the Section 508 Policy implications on IT Asset Management

> Legal requirements

> Due diligent and care in IT asset acquisitions

3

Rehabilitation Act of 1973

- Integral part of American Civil Rights Law
- The spirit of the Rehabilitation Act – "The Rehabilitation Act prohibits discrimination on the basis of disability in programs conducted by Federal agencies, in programs receiving Federal financial assistance, in Federal employment, and in the employment practices of Federal contractors. The standards for determining employment discrimination under the Rehabilitation Act are the same as those used in title I of the Americans with Disabilities Act. (ADA)"
  - ADA Title I Employment - Prohibits discrimination in recruitment, hiring, promotions, training, pay, social activities, and other privileges of employment
- Enforcement processes
  - Complaint
  - Mediation
  - Litigation – Post-hiring, "rights-to-sue" permission is not required from EEOC
- Public law and compliance is mandatory

4

Rehabilitation Act of 1973 and NASA

• Access For People with Disability

- Sections Relevant to NASA
  - » Section 501 requires affirmative action and nondiscrimination in employment by Federal agencies of the executive branch" – Pre-Hiring considerations such as: position descriptions, physical requirements and limitations...
  - » Section 503 requires affirmative action and prohibits employment discrimination by Federal government contractors and subcontractors with contracts of more than $10,000" – Applicable to all federal contracts over the threshold value with the exception of small business
  - » Section 504 requires reasonable accommodations for employees with disabilities; program accessibility; effective communication with people who have hearing or vision disabilities; and accessible new construction and alterations – Post hiring, provide assistive technology, equivalent facilitation or accessible facility with best effort (due diligent and care)
  - » Section 508 requires electronic and information technology accessibility **developed, maintained, procured,** or **used** by the Federal government. Section 508 requires Federal electronic and information technology to be accessible to people with disabilities, including employee and member of the public – Assistive technology procurement and implementations

5

Kennedy Space Center History

- **2005 Agency CIO mandate the all field centers to be compliant with the sections 508 Federal laws**
  - ➤ In 2006, KSC successfully implemented process for accessible EIT procurement
  - ➤ IT Business Office is working on the following issues:
    - » Not-compliant Saturn training materials
    - » Not-compliant Agency form filler solutions
    - » Not-compliant Center Director all-hands meeting video
    - » Not-compliant and not-usable documents posted on KSC WebPages
    - » VoIP phone usability
    - » Signer is not readily visible
    - » WindChill PTC software compliance status
- **January 6, 2011, Mr. Bolden signed NASA Agency Section 508 Policy and it is effective immediately**

Agency Policy Requirements

Section 508 of the Rehabilitation Act of 1973 as amended, requires Federal Agency to provide assistive technology to:

  ➤ Civil servants in the work place.

  ➤ General public interacting with Federal Government.

• **NASA Policy requires KSC developed, maintained, procured, or used information be accessible and usable by all civil servants with disabilities**

• **Applicable to:**

  ➤ WebPages

  ➤ Business, Scientific, Engineering Documents

  ➤ Signer services

  ➤ Videos

  ➤ Software development/acquisition (Highly-Specialized, Business, Database...)

  ➤ Business/Laboratory Equipments

Assistive Technology and Disability Types

- **Screen reader for visual impairments**
  - ➤ Low/No vision, Color Perception
- **Close Caption for hearing loss**
  - ➤ Tone deaf, Deaf
- **Specialized computer hardware for motor skills impairment**
  - ➤ Strength, Control, Paralysis, Prosthesis
- **Specialized video, software for mild cognitive impairments**
  - ➤ Photosensitive Epilepsy, Reading, Memory Processing, Learning, Language…

8

Accessibility Notion

- ## Accessibility = Section 508 Compliance + Usability

  - ### Section 508 Compliance
    - » Meets United States Access Board (USAB) Guidelines and Standards USAB Communication Guidelines and Standards
      - ❖ Electronic and Information Technology Accessibility
      - ❖ Telecommunication Act Accessibility

    - » OR meets NASA policy and defined exceptions
      - ❖ Exception requests will requires legal review before approval

---

Accessibility Notion (Continued)

- **Accessibility = Section 508 Compliance + Usability**
  - ➢ **Usability**
    - » Assistive technology implementation, equivalent facilitation and/or reasonable accommodation that meet's user expectations in performance of his/her work assignment

- **Accessibility space is comprised of these two components: Compliance and Usability**

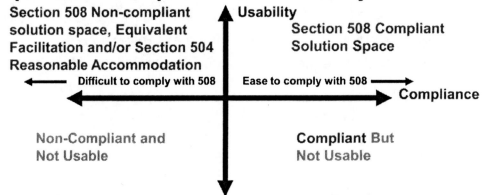

Section 508 Non-compliant solution space, Equivalent Facilitation and/or Section 504 Reasonable Accommodation

Usability
Section 508 Compliant Solution Space

◄—— Difficult to comply with 508   Ease to comply with 508 ——►

Compliance

Non-Compliant and Not Usable

Compliant But Not Usable

Notional View of the Accessibility Space at KSC

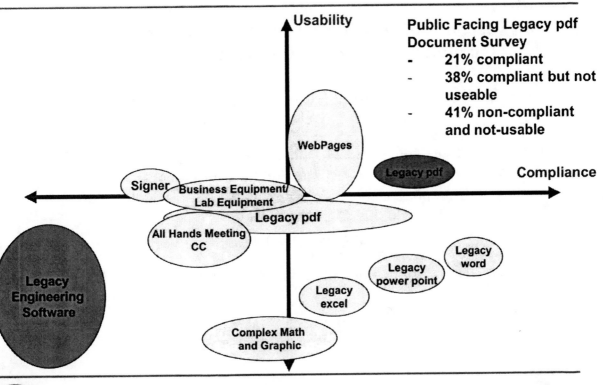

Public Facing Legacy pdf Document Survey
- 21% compliant
- 38% compliant but not useable
- 41% non-compliant and not-usable

Section 508 Applicability to ITAM Activities

- **Section 508 is technical solutions (Assistive Technology) for information accessibilities**

- **Due considerations from ITAM perspectives:**
  - ➤ Procurement assistive technology capable hardware and software
  - ➤ IT services contracts and contract language
  - ➤ Understand the exception and waiver process
  - ➤ Enterprise License Agreements (ELA) and Section 508 compliance due diligence and care
    - ✓ Existing agreements
    - ✓ Future agreements
  - ➤ Due diligence and care documentation (i.e., NF 1707)

IT Asset Management Working Group Meeting

Questions?

Back-up charts

Section 508 Procurement Requirements and Exceptions

- Federal Acquisition Circular (FAC) 97-27, Electronic and Information Technology Accessibility is implemented under FAR Part 39.2
  - ➢ "When Acquiring EIT, agencies must ensure that –
    - (1) Federal employees with disabilities have access to and use of information and data that is comparable to the access and use by the Federal employee who are not individuals with disabilities; and
    - (2) Members of the public with disabilities seeking information or services from an agency have access to and use of information and data that is comparable to the access of to and use of information and data by member of the public who are individual with disabilities.
- Exceptions
  - ➢ Micro-purchase prior to April 1, 2005
  - ➢ Is for a national security system
  - ➢ Is acquired by a contractor incidental to a contract
  - ➢ Is located in a spaces frequented only by service personnel for maintenance, or occasional monitoring equipment
  - ➢ Would impose an undue burden on the Agency
    - » Requires documentation and agency legal counsel to approve
  - ➢ Commercial non-availability
    - » Requires documentation

15

NASA Form 1707 / Section 508 Due Diligence

NASA — National Aeronautics and Space Administration

Special Approvals and Affirmations of Requisitions

CENTER	REQUISITION NUMBER	REQUESTING ORGANIZATION

NAME AND SIGNATURE OF APPROVER	DATE

SECTION 1 — ELECTRONIC AND INFORMATION TECHNOLOGY ACCESSIBILITY (EITAC) SECTION 508

☐ THE PROCUREMENT DOES NOT INCLUDE ELECTRONIC AND INFORMATION TECHNOLOGY (EIT) ITEMS.

OR

☐ THIS PROCUREMENT DOES INCLUDE EIT ITEMS.

AND

☐ THEY MEET THE APPLICABLE ACCESSIBILITY STANDARDS AT 36 CFR Part 1194. *(Attach Market Research Documentation — See PIC 05-01 located at <http://www.hq.nasa.gov/office/procurement/regs/pic05-01.html>)*

OR

☐ IS FOR A COMMERCIAL SUPPLY OR SERVICE AND MARKET RESEARCH HAS DETERMINED THAT SOME OR ALL OF THE APPLICABLE ACCESS BOARD STANDARDS CANNOT BE MET BY SUPPLIES OR SERVICES AVAILABLE IN THE COMMERCIAL MARKET PLACE IN TIME TO SATISFY AGENCY DELIVERY REQUIREMENTS. *(Attach EIT Non-Availability Determination.)*

OR

☐ IS EXEMPT FROM COMPLIANCE WITH APPLICABLE ACCESSIBILITY STANDARDS BASED ON THE FOLLOWING EXCEPTION:

☐ THE ITEM IS FOR A NATIONAL SECURITY SYSTEM;

☐ THE ITEM WILL BE LOCATED IN SPACES FREQUENTED ONLY BY SERVICE PERSONNEL FOR MAINTENANCE, REPAIR OR OCCASIONAL MONITORING OF EQUIPMENT; OR

☐ WOULD IMPOSE AN UNDUE BURDEN ON THE AGENCY. *(Attach Undue Burden Determination.)*

(NOTE: Templates for the determinations noted in this section are attachments to PIC 05-01, available at <http://www.hq.nasa.gov/office/procurement/regs/pic05-01.html>

SECTION 2 — AFFIRMATIVE PROCUREMENT — ENVIRONMENTALLY PREFERABLE PRODUCTS

☐ THE ITEM(S) BEING PURCHASED ARE NOT ON ANY OF THE EPA's COMPREHENSIVE PROCUREMENT GUIDELINE LISTS (CPG) <http://www.epa.gov/epaoswer/non-hw/procure/products.htm>

Case Study of Professor Stephen W. Hawking

- World renown scientist with disabilities
- Information accessibility environment
- Personal information accessibility requirements

Case Study of Professor Stephen W. Hawking

Case Study of Professor Stephen W. Hawking

Case Study of Professor Stephen W. Hawking

- **Professor Hawking**
  - ➢ Suffers from Amyotrophic Lateral Sclerosis (ALS/Lou Gehrig's Disease)
  - ➢ World renown Cosmologist, Mathematician, Physicist and Scholar
  - ➢ Active intellectual life style with ambition for a spaceflight
  - ➢ Closely associated with NASA scientific activities
- **How does Professor Hawking support such active life style?**
  - ➢ Assistive technology and personal assistance to support his active life style

Case Study of Professor Stephen W. Hawking

- **Debilitating conditions of professor Hawking**
  - ➤ Gradually loss of motor skills until complete loss of control
  - ➤ Communicate with increasing slurred speech until 1985, after an emergency tracheotomy ended his ability to speak
  - ➤ After 1985, Professor Hawking could only have small movement of his fingers, head, eye and limited facial expressions
- **Reasonable accommodation for Professor Hawking from 1974 to 1985**
  - ➤ His employer provided him a ground floor house to facilitate better wheelchair access
  - ➤ His research student stay in his house to assist him with some of his daily care and assisted him in his research work. In return, the research student has free housing accommodation and professor Hawking personal guidance in student scientific studies
  - ➤ By 1980, nurses care two hours in the morning and evening at his residence, he communicate with trained assistances
  - ➤ By 1985, he requires 24 hours nursing, he communicated with small gestures such as raising his eyebrows when his assistant points to the correct letter. He had to spell words letter by letter

Case Study of Professor Stephen W. Hawking

- **Assistive Technology and Professor Hawking**
  - ➢ In 1986 "Equalizer" DOS software and word+ replace his spelling cards system
    - » Like -- Promote independent and repaid communication
    - » Like – Write equations and built-up and save lecture materials
    - » Dislike – Desktop application, no mobility
    - » Dislike – No ability to upgrade to Windows OS
  - ➢ With onset of mobile computing and powerful CPU, a laptop with a speech+ synthesizer
    - » Like – More capabilities integrated into mobile environment and most important ability is to speak
    - » Like – Speech synthesizer did not sound like Dalek
    - » Dislike – Speech synthesizer gave him an American accent
  - ➢ Assistive technology gave professor Hawking ability to communicate his scientific ideals to the world.

Provide Accessibility At KSC Environment

- **Disability and Professor Hawking**
  - ➤ "I have had motor neuron disease for practically all my adult life. Yet it has not prevented me from having a very attractive family, and being successful in my work. This is thanks to Jane, my children, and larger number of other people and organizations. I have been lucky, that my condition has progressed more slowly than is often the case. **BUT IT SHOWS THAT ONE NEED NOT LOSE HOPE.**"

- **Assistive Technology will provide hope and path forward to assists people with disabilities to live a more independent and productive lives, as this technology matures.**

CPSIA information can be obtained at www.ICGtesting.com
Printed in the USA
BVOW03s1405181215

430601BV00017B/335/P